# Kids' Travel Guide

# San Francisco

SAN FRANCISCO

**FlyingKids**

Presents:

# KIDS' TRAVEL GUIDE
# SAN FRANCISCO

**Author: Kelsey Fox, Shiela H. Leon**

**Editor: Carma Graber**

**Designer: Slavisa Zivkovic**

**Cover design: Francesca Guido**

**Illustrations: Slavisa Zivkovic, Francesca Guido**

**Published by FlyingKids Limited**

Visit us @ www.theflyingkids.com

Contact us: leonardo@theflyingkids.com

ISBN 978-1-910994-31-3

# TABLE OF CONTENTS

# This is the only page for parents in this book ...

*Dear Parents,*

If you bought this book, you're probably planning a **family trip** with **your kids**.

You are spending **a lot** of time and **money** in the hopes that this family vacation will be pleasant and fun. Of course, you would like your children to get to know the city you are visiting — a little of its **geography**, **local history**, **important sites**, **culture**, **customs**, and more. And you hope they will always remember the trip as a very special experience.

The reality is often quite different. Parents find themselves frustrated as they **struggle to convince** their kids to join a tour or visit a landmark, while the kids just want to stay in and watch TV. Or the kids are glued to their mobile devices and don't pay much attention to the new sights and places of interest. Many parents are disappointed when they return home and discover that their kids don't remember much about the trip and the new things they learned.

That's exactly why the **Kids' Travel Guide** series was created. With the Kids' Travel Guides, young children become researchers and active participants in the trip. During the vacation, kids will read relevant facts about the city you are visiting. The Kids' Travel Guides include **puzzles**, **tasks** to complete, useful **tips**, and **other recommendations** along the way. The kids will meet Leonardo — their tour guide. Leonardo encourages them to **experiment**, **explore**, and be **more involved** in the family's activities—as well as to learn **new information** and make memories throughout the trip. In addition, kids are encouraged to document and write about their experiences during the trip, so that when you return **home**, they will have a **memoir** that will be fun to look at and reread again and again.

The Kids' Travel Guides support children as they get ready for the trip, visit new places, learn new things, and finally, return home. The *Kids' Travel Guide — San Francisco* focuses on **the City by the Bay**. In it, children will find background information on SAN FRANCISCO and its special attractions. The *Kids' Travel Guide — San Francisco* concentrates on 11 central sites that are recommended **for children**. At each of these sites, interesting facts, action items, and **quizzes** await **your kids**.

**You**, the **parents**, are **invited** to participate or to find an available bench and **relax** while you **enjoy** your **active children**. If you are traveling to SAN FRANCISCO, you may also want to get the *Kids' Travel Guide — USA*. It focuses on the country of the United States—its **geography**, **history**, unique **culture**, **traditions**, and **more**—using the **fun** and **interesting** style of the Kids' Travel Guide series.

*Ready for a new experience?*
*Have a nice trip and have fun!*

Leonardo

# Hi, kids!

If you are reading this book, it means you are lucky — you are going to San Francisco!

You may have noticed that your parents are getting ready for the journey. They have bought travel guides, looked for information on the Internet, and printed pages of information. They are talking to friends and people who have already visited San Francisco, in order to learn about it and know what to do, where to go, and when … But this is not just another guidebook for your parents.

**This book is for you only — the young traveler.**

## So what is this book all about?

First and foremost, meet Leonardo, your very own personal guide on this trip. Leonardo has visited many places around the world. (Guess how he got there?) He will be with you throughout the book and the trip. Leonardo will tell you all about the places you will visit … It is always good to learn a little about the city you are visiting and its history beforehand. Leonardo will give you many ideas, quizzes, tips, and other surprises. He will accompany you while you are packing and leaving home. He will stay in the hotel with you (don't worry — it doesn't cost more money)! And he will see the sights with you until you return home.

# A travel diary - the beginning!

# Going to San Francisco!!!

How did you get to San Francisco?

(By plane ✈) / train 🚄 / car 🚗 / other _____

Date of arrival _August 8th_     Time _C.A = 11:30 A.M NY = 2:30 P.M_

Date of departure _August 8th_

All in all, we will stay in San Francisco for _3_ days.

Is this your first visit? (YES) NO

Where will you sleep?

(In a hotel) / in a campsite / in an apartment / other _____

What sites are you planning to visit?
_Alcatraz, John Muir Woods, Horse Castle, Wine store, Fisherman's wharf._

What special activities are you planning to do?
_Cable Cars, Cable Car museum, fortune cookie factory, Fuller House House, lombard St._

Are you excited about the trip?

This is an excitement indicator. Ask your family members how excited they are (from "not at all" up to "very, very much"), and mark each of their answers on the indicator. Leonardo has already marked the level of his excitement ...

very, very much

not at all

Leonardo

# WHO IS TRAVELING?

Write down the names of the family members traveling with you and their answers to the questions.

**PASTE A PICTURE OF YOUR FAMILY.**

Name: ME! (Emma.S.)

Age: 10

Has he or she visited San Francisco before? yes / (no)

What is the most exciting thing about your upcoming trip?
Alcatraz, and the Fuller House House.

Name: Mary

Age: 42

Has he or she visited San Francisco before? yes / (no)

What is the most exciting thing about your upcoming trip?

Name: Dan

Age: 42

Has he or she visited San Francisco before? yes / (no)

What is the most exciting thing about your upcoming trip?
Lumbard St.

Name: Thomas

Age: 17

Has he or she visited San Francisco before? yes / (no)

What is the most exciting thing about your upcoming trip?

Name: Aunt Linda

Age: 59

Has he or she visited San Francisco before? (yes) / no

What is the most exciting thing about your upcoming trip?

# Preparations at home – do not forget …!

Mom or Dad will take care of packing clothes (how many pairs of pants, which comb to take …). So Leonardo will only tell you about the stuff he thinks you may want to bring along to San Francisco.

Here's the Packing List Leonardo made for you. You can check off each item as you pack it:

▦ *Kids' Travel Guide — San Francisco* — of course!

▦ Comfortable walking shoes

▦ A raincoat (One that folds up is best — sometimes it rains without warning …)

▦ A hat (and sunglasses, if you want)

▦ Pens and pencils

▦ Crayons and markers (It is always nice to color and paint.)

▦ A notebook or writing pad (You can use it for games or writing, or to draw or doodle in when you're bored …)

▦ A book to read

▦ Your smartphone/tablet or camera

## Pack your things in a small bag (or backpack). You may also want to take these things:

- Snacks, fruit, candy, and chewing gum. If you are flying, it can help a lot during takeoff and landing, when there's pressure in your ears.

- Some games you can play while sitting down: electronic games, booklets of crossword puzzles, connect-the-numbers, etc.

Now let's see if you can find 12 items you should take on a trip in this word search puzzle:

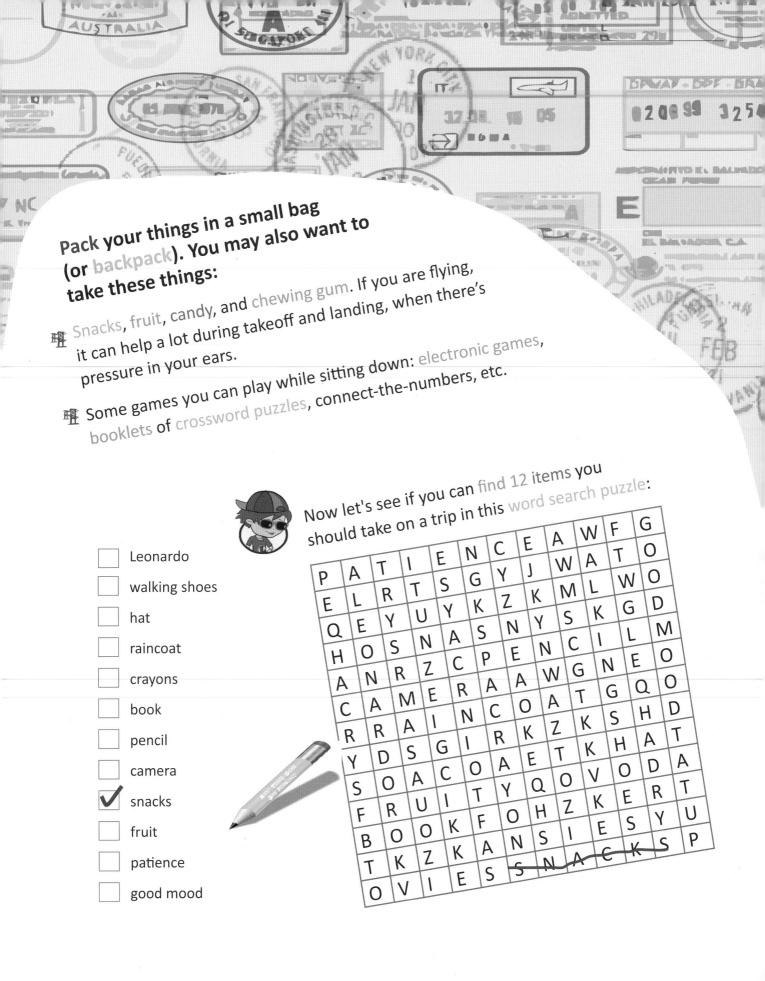

- [ ] Leonardo
- [ ] walking shoes
- [ ] hat
- [ ] raincoat
- [ ] crayons
- [ ] book
- [ ] pencil
- [ ] camera
- [✓] snacks
- [ ] fruit
- [ ] patience
- [ ] good mood

| P | A | T | I | E | N | C | E | A | W | F | G |
|---|---|---|---|---|---|---|---|---|---|---|---|
| E | L | R | T | S | G | Y | J | W | A | T | O |
| Q | E | Y | U | Y | K | Z | K | M | L | W | O |
| H | O | S | N | A | S | N | Y | S | K | G | D |
| A | N | R | Z | C | P | E | N | C | I | L | M |
| C | A | M | E | R | A | A | W | G | N | E | O |
| R | R | A | I | N | C | O | A | T | G | Q | O |
| Y | D | S | G | I | R | K | Z | K | S | H | D |
| S | O | A | C | O | A | E | T | K | H | A | T |
| F | R | U | I | T | Y | Q | O | V | O | D | A |
| B | O | O | K | F | O | H | Z | K | E | R | T |
| T | K | Z | K | A | N | S | I | E | S | Y | U |
| O | V | I | E | S | S | N | A | C | K | S | P |

# San Francisco, California: The City by the Bay

San Francisco is a big city in the big state of California! California sits on the West Coast of the United States of America. It borders the states of Oregon, Nevada, and Arizona, and the country of Mexico. But California's biggest border is its coastline that touches the Pacific Ocean.

Help Leonardo find California on the map of the United States.

Can you also help him find how many neighboring states California has? _____

## Quizzes!

Which two states are bigger than California? Use the map as a clue!

_____

ANSWER
Texas and Alaska are bigger.

In terms of size, California is only the third largest state. But it has more people than any other state in America!

# The Golden State

Every state in the United States has a nickname. California's nickname is "The Golden State."

Can you think why California has this nickname? If you don't already know, you'll find the answer somewhere on this page ...

Does **your** state or country have a nickname? What is it?

A few more things about California ...
The Capital: Sacramento
What is the capital of **your** state or country? _____

State Motto: "Eureka!" meaning "*I Have Found It*!"
Do you know what they found? G_ _ _!
What is the motto of your state or country? _____

State Song: "*I Love You, California*"
What is the song of your state or country? _____

## San Francisco, here we come!

San Francisco, the fourth largest city in California, is one of the most beautiful cities in the world! It is situated on a natural harbor called San Francisco Bay. The city is known for its steep hills, beautiful parks, different styles of architecture, historic cable cars, and excellent food!

### Where did San Francisco get its name?

When the Spanish first came to California, they called this area *Yerba Buena*. That's Spanish for "Good Grass" or "Good Herbs." In 1848, the name was changed to San Francisco to honor Saint Francis.

# What does San Francisco look like?

Here is a map of the city.
If you look closely, you can see that San Francisco is divided into different sections. These sections are called neighborhoods.

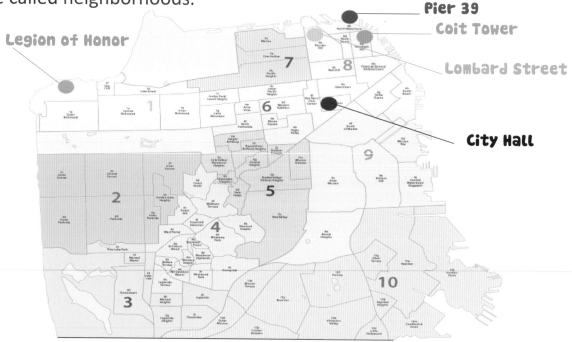

**Legion of Honor**

**Pier 39**

**Coit Tower**

**Lombard Street**

**City Hall**

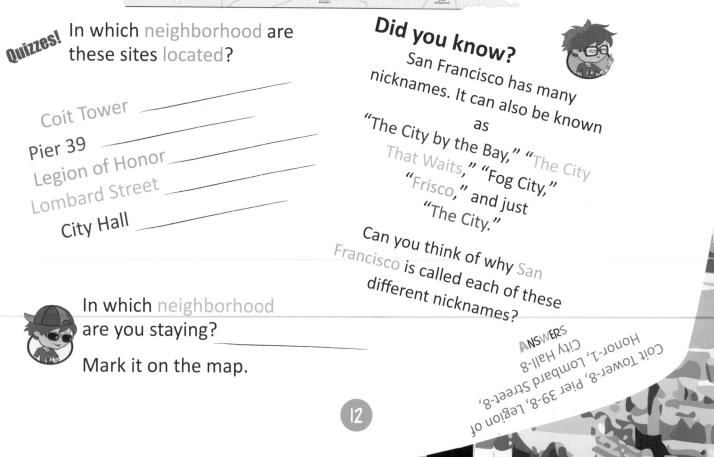

**Quizzes!** In which neighborhood are these sites located?

Coit Tower _____

Pier 39 _____

Legion of Honor _____

Lombard Street _____

City Hall _____

In which neighborhood are you staying? _____

Mark it on the map.

## Did you know?

San Francisco has many nicknames. It can also be known as "The City by the Bay," "The City That Waits," "Fog City," "Frisco," and just "The City."

Can you think of why San Francisco is called each of these different nicknames?

# Gold Rush

## San Francisco and the gold Rush

Native Americans lived in the area that is now San Francisco for hundreds of years, but it did not become a real city until the Spanish arrived. When the city became San Francisco, only 469 people lived there! They included Ohlone Indians, Spanish Californians, Hawaiians, Europeans, South Americans, and New Zealanders.

San Francisco's population stayed small until 1849. That's when the Gold Rush started! James Marshall found gold at Sutter's Mill! When word got out, thousands of people rushed to California. They wanted to find gold, too, and "strike it rich!" These people were called forty-niners. Can you guess why? Though most of them were Americans, others came from China, Mexico, Europe, and Australia. The Gold Rush only lasted three years. Even when all the gold was gone, many forty-niners decided to stay in California.

### Did you know?
Denim jeans were invented in San Francisco during the Gold Rush. Denim was first used as a thick material that was perfect for making tents to sleep in. But Levi Strauss noticed that the miners needed durable pants that would hold up while they worked. Denim pants (and Levi's) have been popular ever since!

# Things you'll see only in San Francisco

Crooked streets, beautiful parks and gardens, cultural neighborhoods — there are plenty of attractions in San Francisco for you to see.

Now it's time for Leonardo to lend a hand! He has gathered information about the most popular sites and activities.

Sourdough bread. The yeast needed to make sourdough bread only grows in San Francisco — and the city has made this tasty bread famous! Try a sandwich on sourdough, or eat soup out of a bowl made of sourdough.

## Have you noticed the many heart-shaped statues?

Every year, different artists paint or decorate big heart-shaped statues. Then they place the statues in different spots around the city. At the end of the year, the statues are auctioned off to raise money for charity! The statues are always in different places, so keep your eyes peeled! If you find a heart statue, take a picture of it.

Be sure to write down where you found it!

_____

_____

_____

# Getting around in
## San Francisco

*There are several fun ways to travel around San Francisco.*

One way to get around is by trolley.

The trolleys can take you just about anywhere in the city. They stop frequently and move slowly, so there are plenty of opportunities for you to take pictures of the things you see! San Francisco is one of the few cities left in the world that still uses old-fashioned trolley cars. The city brought old trolleys from all over the world to use here in San Francisco.

 When you see a trolley, can you tell where it is from? Write it down!

You can also get around on San Francisco's metro system called MUNI (pronounced like "*myoo-nee*"). MUNI runs underneath San Francisco's streets. It can get you very close to many popular places, so you won't have to walk very far.

 Can you think of one advantage and one disadvantage to using MUNI to sightsee?

Advantage _____

Disadvantage _____

Why is it called MUNI? MUNI is short for San Francisco MUNIcipal Railway. "Municipal" means it belongs to the city.

# The famous Cable cars!

The most famous way to travel in San Francisco is on a cable car! Cable cars are a good way to get from one end of the city to the other. They also make it much easier to get up those big hills! You will likely have to wait in a long line to ride on the cable car, but it's worth it!

## Quizzes!

Can you guess how fast the cable car travels?

a. Nine miles per hour (14.5 km/hour)

b. Three miles per hour (4.8 km/hour)

c. Five miles per hour (8 km/hour)

## Tip!

Try to get a seat up front, and ask the cable car conductor to ring the bells!

If you want to learn more about San Francisco's cable cars, and even see the famous pulleys that make them move, visit the Cable Car Museum. It's free!

The cable car is a great way to travel from Union Square to Fisherman's Wharf! Take the Powell-Hyde line for the most scenic route! **As you ride over the hills and through the streets, mark on the map what you see.**

Powell & Market

Gates of Chinatown

Union Square

Lombard Street

Ghirardelli Square

Fisherman's Wharf

Telegraph Hill & Coit Tower
(in the distance!)

Alcatraz
(In distance!)

# The heart of San Francisco ...
## Union Square

Union Square is the bustling heart of San Francisco!

Locals and tourists alike come to Union Square to go shopping. During the holidays, a big Christmas tree and a big menorah are lit up. An ice-skating rink is set up in the center of the square for people to enjoy.

Union Square wasn't always as luxurious as it is now. During the Gold Rush, it was called Morton Street. It was famous for its saloons and gambling halls. In fact, Morton Street was such a bad area that even the police were scared to go there.

## Did you know?

San Francisco was nowhere near the fighting during the American Civil War between the Union and the Confederates. But Union Square got its name because it was once used for rallies to support the Union Army.

Stand in the middle of Union Square facing Macy's. What do you see?

On the left: _____

In front: _____

Behind you: _____

On the right: _____

Answers

ON THE RIGHT: The Westin St. Francis Hotel

BEHIND YOU: Saks Fifth Avenue;

IN FRONT OF YOU: Macy's windows and The Cheesecake Factory;

ON THE LEFT: Neiman-Marcus;

# Union Square – a special place

Today, Union Square has many fancy restaurants and hotels. Stores like Louis Vuitton and Prada make it a world-famous spot for shopping! Many people who live in San Francisco come to Union Square for a special night on the town. They eat dinner at a nice restaurant, and then go to one of the many nearby theaters.

My impressions of Union Square: _____

Which is the most beautiful building? _____

Did we buy anything? If so, what? _____

How did we spend our time in Union Square? _____

_____

**Tip!**

For great views of San Francisco, go into the Westin St. Francis Hotel and ride the glass elevators. If you lean your head against the glass, you can see the whole city.

# Chinatown ...

*A Chinese neighborhood inside San Francisco*

Visiting Chinatown is like taking a small jump into China. During the Gold Rush, many Chinese immigrants moved into this one section of the city. They wanted a place where they could continue their Chinese traditions and feel as if they were back home. Today, Chinatown feels a lot like it did during the Gold Rush! Of course, even tourists are invited to visit and enjoy. When you enter Chinatown, you'll notice new smells, tastes, music, and colors! Chinatown feels different than the rest of San Francisco.

Do you hear people speaking Chinese on the streets? Have you noticed all of the different street signs? They're written in Chinese!

## Did you know?

Do you notice the interesting roofs on many of Chinatown's buildings? They look like they have several roofs sitting on top of each other. These buildings are called pagodas. It is believed that they keep spirits (ghosts) from climbing into the houses, because the spirits will trip on the curved edges of the roof.

Pass through the Dragon Gate and enter Chinatown. It's a must-see for visitors to San Francisco! It is the most popular place for tourists to visit in the whole city. It attracts more tourists than even the Golden Gate Bridge!

19

# 唐人街

## FestiVals in Chinatown

### A Party in Chinatown!

Chinatown is almost always busy, but it's especially busy during festival time. In January or February, San Francisco has a big street fair and parade to celebrate the Chinese New Year. Every autumn, they celebrate the Autumn Moon Festival. People eat lots of food, especially moon cakes—moon-shaped pastries with a sweet filling.

**Tip!**

Most tourists just stay on Grant Avenue, Chinatown's "main street," but it's worth it to explore some side streets.

### Did you know?

The Fortune Cookie Factory in Ross Alley makes over 20,000 cookies per day!

### Did you know?

Chinatown in San Francisco has the largest Chinese population in the world outside of Asia!

Leonardo wrote his name in Chinese. Can you write like him?

萊昂納多

Have you ever visited a cookie factory? Find Ross Alley and go to the Fortune Cookie Factory.

# Things to do in Chinatown

Chinatown is a great place to learn about Chinese culture! Do you know what a Chinese lantern looks like?

**Quizzes!** Which one of the pictures is a Chinese lantern?

 **A**   **B**   **C**

ANSWER
A

A few things to do in Chinatown — check off the things you do!

○ Visit a Chinese restaurant or snack stand and try one new food you might enjoy. What did you try?

_____

○ Count the dragons! How many dragons did you find?

_____

○ Take a picture of a cricket in a cage.

○ Greet a Chinese person by saying "Ni-hao!" ("Hello!" It's pronounced like Nee-how.)

○ Try a freshly baked fortune cookie.

○ Pick up a souvenir. What did you get?

_____

# The Golden Gate Bridge

The Golden Gate Bridge is one of the most famous images in the world.

**A** GOLDEN **IDEA!**

In the 1930s, San Franciscans wanted an easier way to connect the two sides of the San Francisco Bay.

For many years, San Franciscans tried to find a better way to get from the city of San Francisco to Marin — but engineers claimed a bridge would be impossible to build or too expensive.

Only one engineer, Joseph Strauss, believed there was a way to connect the two sides of the bay. Not only did he build a new kind of bridge, he did so at an affordable cost.

**Quizzes!**

**How long is the Golden Gate Bridge?**

a. 1 mile (1.6 km)

b. 1.7 miles (2.7 km)

c. 10 miles (16 km)

d. 2.5 miles (4 km)

For four years, thousands of designers and construction workers worked to build this beautiful bridge. Finally, the Golden Gate Bridge opened to the public in May 1937. Since then, nearly 1.5 billion people have crossed it!

ANSWER
b

# Interesting facts about the Golden Gate Bridge

The Golden Gate Bridge is 1.7 miles long (1,970 meters). When it first opened, it was the longest suspension bridge in the world! But 30 years later, a longer bridge was built in New York.

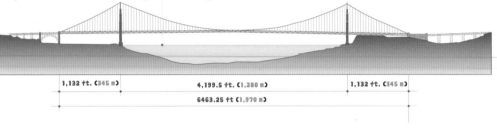

## A few things not everyone knows about the Golden Gate Bridge:

- The bridge was supposed to be painted yellow with black stripes so that ships would be able to see it in fog. Luckily for us, not everyone thought this was a good idea. The official color of the bridge is not gold. The color is called "Golden Gate International Orange."

- The term Golden Gate refers to the Golden Gate Strait, which connects the bay to the Pacific Ocean.

- Eleven men died building the Golden Gate Bridge.

- When construction ended in May 1937, Chief Engineer Joseph B. Strauss wrote a poem titled "The Mighty Task Is Done." It is written somewhere on the Bridge.

- The bridge is especially designed to move! A swinging bridge might sound scary, but it actually means the bridge won't break when the earth shakes.

- A group of 50 employees and painters maintain the bridge.

- Each week, they use 1,057 gallons (or about 4,000 liters) of paint!

 If there is time, you can walk or ride a bike all the way across the bridge!

# Fisherman's Wharf & Pier 39

The city of San Francisco was built around the natural harbor of San Francisco Bay. The harbor is still a busy place! Ships and boats come and go from Pier 39, and tourists wander around the waterfront marketplaces at Fisherman's Wharf. It's easy to lose track of time here because there are so many things to see!

The nearby Aquarium of the Bay will give you a "diver's-eye" view of sea life in the San Francisco Bay. You can walk through clear tunnels to see fish, sharks, and other creatures.

The Venetian Carousel was carved and painted in Italy, but it's the only carousel in the US painted with images of its home city.

**Can you guess how many people visit Fisherman's Wharf every year?**

a. 1 million

Quizzes!

b. 1 billion

c. 15 million

d. 10 million

ANSWER
c

San Francisco is famous for its seafood and sourdough bread, both of which come from Fisherman's Wharf. What do you think of Fisherman's Wharf?

Smelly _____ Yummy _____ Crowded _____ Cool! _____

# The sea lions of Pier 39

Usually, sea lions and other marine animals live on small islands just off San Francisco's coast. But after the big Loma Prieta earthquake of 1989, sea lions started hanging out at Pier 39. The city of San Francisco embraced the sea lions, and they are now a famous symbol of Pier 39!

### Did you know?
The San Francisco Bay is not actually a bay. A bay is filled with ocean water. San Francisco Bay is really an estuary, which means it has a mix of fresh water and ocean water. It is the largest estuary on the West Coast of the United States.

As you may have noticed, sea lions are very talkative. They say exactly what is on their minds. Listen to the sea lions and try to make the **ARK! ARK! ARK!** sound that they are making. Do you sound like a sea lion? Maybe one of them will even answer you!

Why do seagulls fly over the sea?

## Tip!
Love the sea lions? Pay a quick visit to the Sea Lion Center to learn more about them.

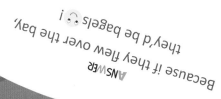

ANSWER
Because if they flew over the bay, they'd be bagels! 😊

# All things sea lion ...

### Did you know?

There are more sea lions at Pier 39 in the winter than in the summer. During the summer months, the sea lions migrate south to the Channel Islands to breed.

**Spend a few minutes watching the sea lions. What kinds of things are they doing? How many are there?**

_____

_____

_____

### Fun facts about sea lions

Sea lions are special mammals who can live in both the water and on land. The sea lions at Pier 39 sleep on their docks, but they'll go swimming when they want to eat.

Do you see any sea lions swimming?

A sea lion can swim up to 30 miles (48 kilometers) an hour! When they want to swim very fast, they glide on the surface of the water.

A baby sea lion is called a pup.

Are there any pups at Pier 39?

Sea lions can live to be 30 years old. That's a long time for an ocean animal.

# See the street performers!

**When you're ready to leave the sea lions,
walk back to the main street in front of Pier 39.**

You are probably seeing a lot of street performers as you walk around Fisherman's Wharf and Pier 39! Many aspiring magicians, puppeteers, dancers, and even human statues come here to test out their acts in front of tourists!

 Write down all of the interesting street performers you see so that you will remember them. You can even take a picture of some of your favorites.

Funniest street performer: _____

Scariest street performer: _____

Strangest street performer: _____

My favorite street performer: _____

# Exploring Alcatraz

Alcatraz has been a lighthouse island and a bird sanctuary, but it is most famous for being a prison! Until the mid-1900s, Alcatraz was a place for the most dangerous of all prisoners. Al Capone, George "Machine Gun" Kelly, and the "Birdman" all spent time in Alcatraz. Today, you can take a boat from Pier 39 to Alcatraz Island and take a tour of the **prison**!

 **Sometimes the weather on** Alcatraz Island is colder or windier than in the city. Be sure to dress in layers and wear comfortable shoes.

 **Did you know?**
When Alcatraz was a **prison**, there were many children who lived on the island. They lived there because their fathers were prison guards. Many of them had to take a boat to school every day. They had to follow many rules, like "No toy guns." Can you imagine living in a place like Alcatraz?

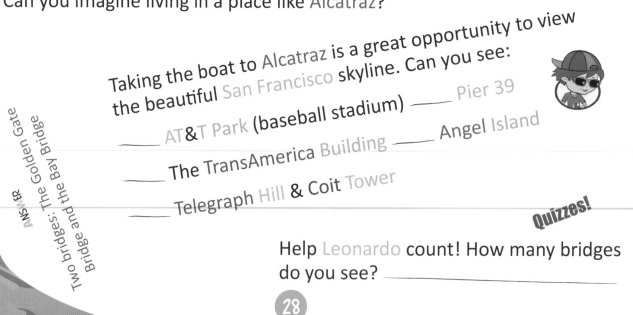

Taking the boat to Alcatraz is a great opportunity to view the beautiful San Francisco skyline. Can you see:

____ AT&T Park (baseball stadium)    ____ Pier 39

____ The TransAmerica Building  ____ Angel Island

____ Telegraph Hill & Coit Tower

**Quizzes!**

Help Leonardo count! How many bridges do you see? _____

# Prison life in Alcatraz

On your tour of Alcatraz, you'll see prisoners' cells, the mess hall, library, and "dark holes." Dark holes were where prisoners went when they got in trouble!

 Find a cell and look inside. What do you see? Find eight items from the cell in the word search below:

Words you can find are:
blanket, toilet, mirror, shelf, matches, sink, comb, bed, ~~chess~~, paints

Which of these items would be most important to you?

```
B  D  S  S  S  D  T  C
M  G  T  I  E  E  O  H
O  L  N  B  K  F  I  E
C  K  I  N  E  X  L  S
N  M  A  T  C  H  E  S
H  L  P  H  Q  I  T  X
B  R  O  R  R  I  M  R
S  H  E  L  F  J  X  G
```

## Did you know?

Alcatraz is named after a bunch of birds! Long before it was a prison, Juan de Ayala of Spain discovered the island in 1775. He named it *Las Isla de Los Alcatraces*, or "Pelican Island."

**Quizzes!** How many people successfully escaped from Alcatraz?

a. 30     b. 0     c. 1     d. 10

ANSWER

b. 0. About 60 people were caught trying to escape Alcatraz Island. Three people successfully made it off the island, but drowned trying to swim away.

# North Beach - Little Italy

North Beach isn't actually a beach! It is a neighborhood famous for its Italian culture. That's why its nickname has become "Little Italy." In the early 1900s, many Italians made this neighborhood their home. During the 1906 earthquake, the Italians in Little Italy used barrels of red wine to put out the fire and save nearby Telegraph Hill!

Did you notice that the colors of the Italian flag are painted on each street lamp? Add the Italian colors onto the street lamp below!

What other Italian things do you see in North Beach?

_____

_____

## Add the Italian decor

**Did you know?**
The same Grant Avenue you walked along in Chinatown is here in North Beach. This very long street is the oldest street in San Francisco. It is the heart of both Chinatown and Little Italy.

# Telegraph Hill & Coit Tower

*What does Coit Tower look like to you?*
Does it look like a fire hose? Some people say Coit Tower was built as a monument to the firefighters who spent three days trying to put out fires after the 1906 earthquake. This is a nice story, but the tower's resemblance to a fire hose wasn't planned. The tower was built in 1931 with money left by Lillie Hitchcock Coit. She wanted her fortune to go to keeping San Francisco beautiful.

Inside the tower, you'll see murals painted by famous San Francisco artists. These murals show life during the Great Depression, when people were very poor. They can tell us a lot about how people lived then.

Coit Tower has some of the best views in San Francisco. Take the old-fashioned elevator to the top to see a 360-degree view of the city and the bay. What sites do you see?

_____ TransAmerica Building _____ Alcatraz _____ Golden Gate Bridge _____ Bay Bridge _____ Lombard Street _____ Pier 39

**Did you know?**
There are about 200 wild parrots who live on Telegraph Hill. It's not clear how they got there, but the cherry-headed conures and blue-crowned conures are now a famous part of San Francisco. See if you can spot some!

# Golden Gate Park

Of all of the city parks in the United States, Golden Gate Park is one of the biggest! It's been around since the 1860s, when San Franciscans began to feel the need for a nice park like New Yorkers had in Central Park. Today, Golden Gate Park has museums, lakes, playgrounds, gardens, and much more! As you spend the day exploring the park, check off the things you see.

_____ Dutch Windmill _____ Bison _____ The AIDS Memorial Grove

_____ Horseshoe Pits _____ Japanese Tea Gardens

_____ The Carousel _____ Botanical Gardens

We had lunch at _____

Museums we visited: _____

My favorite site(s) in the park: _____

**Did you know?**
Golden Gate Park was once a big, free-range zoo! Today, the only animals left are the herds of bison in the Buffalo Paddock.

**Tip!**
Rent a rowboat and paddle along the big lake in the middle of the park. Strawberry Island is fun to play on and a great place for a picnic!

# The Japanese Tea Gardens

The Japanese Tea Gardens have been around since the California Mid-Winter Exposition in 1894. A few years after the Exposition, master gardener Makoto Hagiwara made the gardens even bigger and more impressive! This is now a beautiful, quiet oasis in the middle of the big city.

To fully experience the Japanese Tea Gardens:

_____ Cross over a traditional drum bridge.

_____ Try a warm cup of Japanese tea.

_____ Enjoy a fortune cookie.

_____ Find the bronze Buddha statue.

_____ Choose a hill and climb it to explore.

_____ Feed the koi fish in the koi ponds.

**Tip!** Find the bronze Buddha statue. Sitting among all of the plants and flowers is a bronze statue that is 10 $\frac{1}{2}$ feet (3.2 meters) tall. This Buddha was made almost 200 years ago! The actual name of this statue is *Amazarashi-No-Hotoke*, which means "Buddha who sits through sunny and rainy weather without shelter." Can you think of why the statue has this long name?

### Did you know?

Makoto Hagiwara, the master gardener who made the Tea Gardens so beautiful, is also credited with inventing the fortune cookie!

33

# Lombard **Street**

San Francisco has 43 hills, but Lombard Street is easily the most famous!

Lombard Street is often called the "crookedest" and the "steepest" street in the city, but actually it isn't. Vermont Avenue is the crookedest, and Filbert Street is the steepest.

## Quizzes!

At which cross street do Lombard Street's curves begin? _____

At which cross street do they end? _____

Hundreds of cars line up every day to drive down Lombard Street and experience the hairpin turns for themselves.

## Did you know?

Lombard Street has appeared in many famous movies, television shows, and even video games. The most famous movie it's in is the classic film "Vertigo," by Alfred Hitchcock.

Did your family drive down Lombard Street? How many turns did you count?

# Quizzes

Use the hints to guess what these famous things found in San Francisco are.

I. If you take my elevator up 16 stories, you can see the entire city of San Francisco! If you walk through my lobby, you will get a glimpse of San Francisco's past.

What am I? _____

2. We love to summer in San Francisco because it is nice and warm. We lounge around Pier 39, and only get up to go swimming and eat. Sometimes we are very loud, but the thousands of people who come to visit us do not seem to mind!

Who are we? _____

3. Today, I am known for expensive shopping and fancy restaurants. But during the Gold Rush, people came to me to drink and gamble, and even policemen were scared to visit me. I am much happier today!

What am I? _____

ANSWERS

1- Coit Tower, 2- The sea lions, 3- Union Square

San Francisco Trivia!

I. Which famous article of clothing was invented in San Francisco?

      a. Dresses  b. Galoshes  c. Denim jeans  d. Toe socks

2. San Francisco is famous for this kind of bread:

      a. Sourdough  b. Wheat  c. Rye  d. Pumpkin

3. What is the oldest street in all of San Francisco?

      a. Grant Avenue  b. Sutter Street
    c. Lombard Street  d. 22nd Street

ANSWERS
1-c, 2-a, 3-a

# A San Francisco Crossword

## ACROSS

2. A baby sea lion
3. _____ Tower
4. The famous jeans Levi Strauss invented
7. Where you'll find the Fortune Cookie Factory
8. Statue in the Japanese Tea Garden

## DOWN

1. The state in which you'll find San Francisco
2. Telegraph Hill's tree-dwellers
3. _____ cars
5. San Francisco has 43
6. Sourdough is a type of _____

# Can you break the code?

*Use the key below to decipher Leonardo's journal entry about his trip to San Francisco*

**Q = A**     **Z = O**     **M = E**     **J = I**

I had a great time in SQN FRQNCJSCZ (_ _ _  _ _ _ _ _ _ _ _)! I ate lots of Ghirardelli chocolate and SZURDZUGH (_ _ _ _ _ _ _ _ _) bread. I rode the CQBLM CQR (_ _ _ _ _  _ _ _) and even got to ring the bell as we passed Lombard Street. At Fisherman's Wharf, we saw lots of street performers, and I got to ride the CQRZUSML (_ _ _ _ _ _ _ _).

My favorite thing in San Francisco was Pier 39 and the SMQ LJZNS (_ _ _  _ _ _ _ _). Then again, I also loved the PQRRZTS (_ _ _ _ _ _ _) on Telegraph Hill and the shopping in UNJZN SqUQRM (_ _ _ _ _  _ _ _ _ _ _) and Chinatown. I guess I loved MVMRYTHJNG (_ _ _ _ _ _ _ _ _ _) about the beautiful City by the Bay!

## UNSCRAMBLE THE FAMOUS SAN FRANCISCO SITES

Gldone eaGt rkaP _____

ireP 93 _____

ioBsn docadkP _____

nonUi qeuSar _____

aaztclrA _____

sFrnaihme's aWfrh _____

dmraLob eStrte _____

# SUMMARY OF THE TRIP

*We had great fun, what a pity it is over ...*

**Which** places **did you** visit? _____

**Whom did you** meet...

Did you meet tourists from other countries? **Yes / No**
If you did meet tourists, where did they come from?
(Name their nationalities): _____

**Shopping** and souvenirs...

What did you buy on the trip? _____

What did you want to buy, but ended up not buying?

## Experiences

What are the most memorable experiences of the trip?

_____

_____

_____

_____

# AND TO SUM IT ALL UP...

**What were the most beautiful places and the best experiences of your journey?**

> First place –

> Second place –

> Third place –

And now,

a difficult tasks — talk with your family and decide:

**What did everyone enjoy most on the trip?**

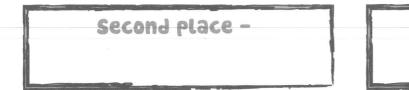

> Grand Prize –

39

# A journal

| Date | What did we do? |
| --- | --- |
| | |
| | |
| | |
| | |
| | |
| | |
| | |
| | |
| | |
| | |
| | |

# A journal

| Date | What did we do? |
| --- | --- |
| _____ | _____ |
| _____ | _____ |
| _____ | _____ |
| _____ | _____ |
| _____ | _____ |
| _____ | _____ |
| _____ | _____ |
| _____ | _____ |
| _____ | _____ |
| _____ | _____ |
| _____ | _____ |

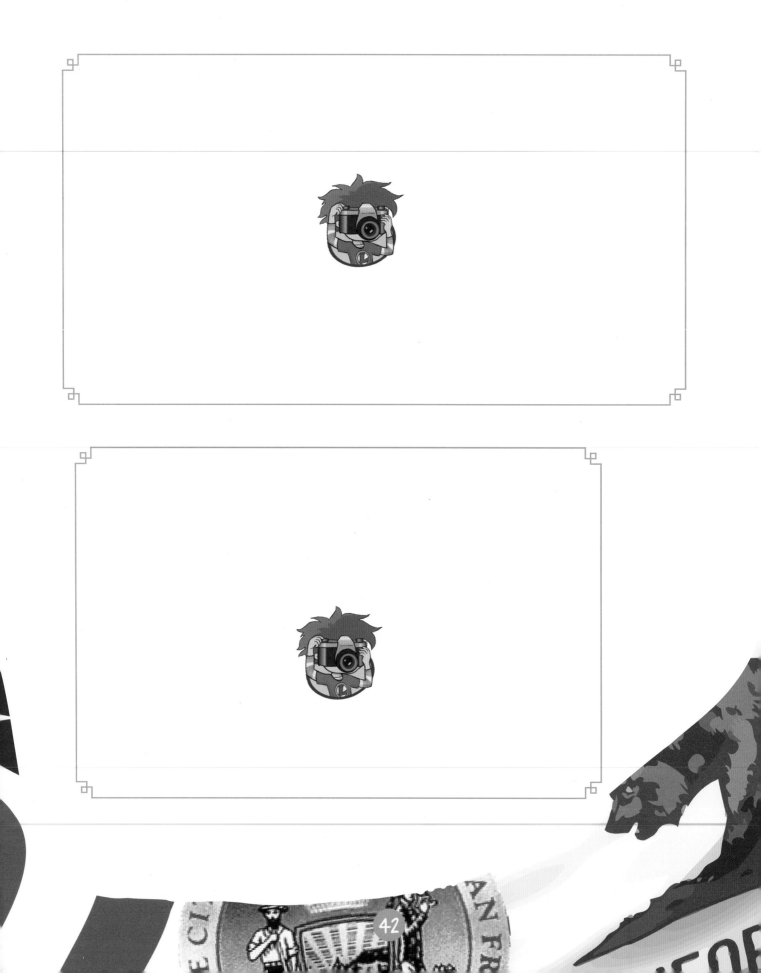

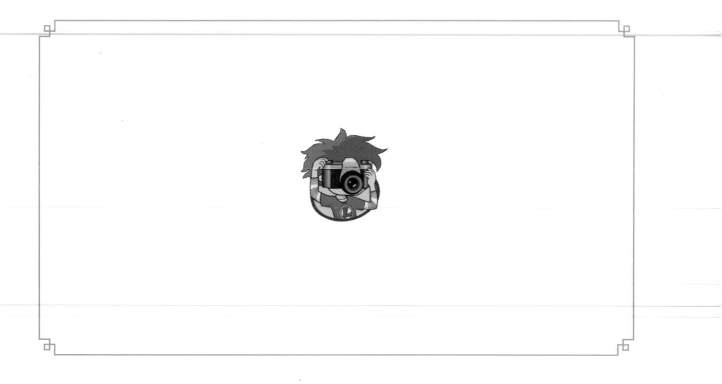

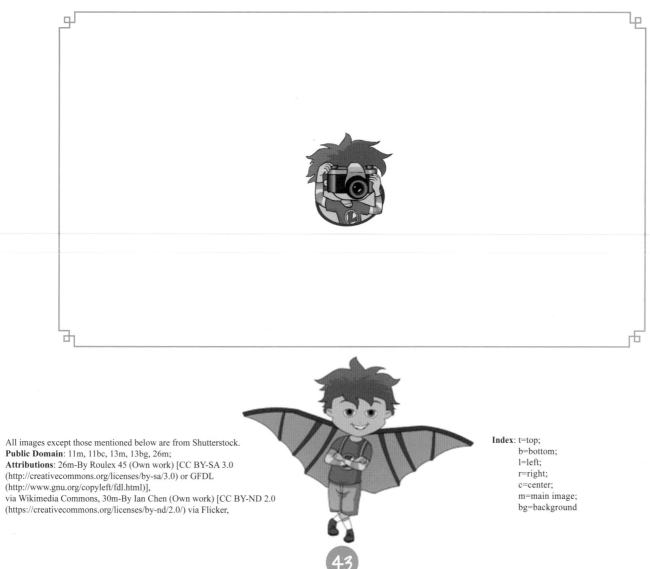

**Index**: t=top;
b=bottom;
l=left;
r=right;
c=center;
m=main image;
bg=background

# ENJOY MORE FUN ADVENTURES WITH LEONARDO AND FlyingKids

## ITALY

## THAILAND

## JAPAN

## FRANCE

## GERMANY    SPAIN    AUSTRALIA    CHINA

## USA

### SPECIAL EDITIONS

## UNITED KINGDOM

## KIDS' ACTIVITY BOOK SERIES

**AGES 4-8**

# FOR FREE DOWNLOADS OF MORE ACTIVITIES, GO TO
# WWW.THEFLYINGKIDS.COM